Presented to:

_____

From:

_____

Date:

_____

Quiet Moments with God

DEVOTIONAL

Honor Books
Tulsa, Oklahoma

Quiet Moments with God Devotional
ISBN 1-56292-792-2
Copyright 2001 © by Honor Books
P.O. Box 55388
Tulsa, Oklahoma 74155
Second Printing

Devotionals drawn from *Quiet Moments with God Devotional* series, including *Breakfast with God, Coffee Break with God, Daybreak with God, In the Garden with God, In the Kitchen with God, Sunset with God, Tea Time with God, Through the Night with God,* and *Christmas with God,* all published by Honor Books.

Introduction

We rush through our days like Olympic athletes pushing their bodies—and minds and spirits—to the limit. We pack thirty hours into our twenty-four-hour schedules, and usually our to-do lists exceed our ability to accomplish everything. Juggling work, family, community, church, and other commitments can often be so frustrating that the simple pleasures and the joy of living get lost in the shuffle.

But it doesn't have to be that way.

Taking time for quiet moments with God is more than a pause that refreshes. It can be a lifeline for survival.

Throughout Scripture, God encourages His children to draw near to Him, to come and experience His love and grace, to take shelter in His arms, to seek Him, to know Him, to trust in Him. His loving invitation to enter into His presence knows no boundaries of time or space or schedule or place. Believers throughout history have found joy and peace in His presence. Wherever you are, no matter what time of day, you can spend devotional moments with God.

Quiet time spent in prayer and reflection can be the most important part of your day. Whether you're a morning person or a night owl, a mother or an executive, a senior or a teen, you can meet with God and be refreshed by His presence and renewed by His tender love.

This beautiful new edition of *Quiet Moments with God* will help you find the heavenly focus you need for living. Let the beautiful illustrations delight your eyes. May the words of comfort and joy inspire your heart.

A quiet moment with God is the *best* part of the day.

THE LORD GOD FORMED MAN OF THE
DUST OF THE GROUND, AND BREATHED INTO HIS
NOSTRILS THE BREATH OF LIFE.

GENESIS 2:7 NKJV

Take a Breather

The fast-paced, relentless duties of life often cause us to say with a sigh, "I need a breather." Medical researchers have discovered that for virtually every person who does any type of work, performance level improves when a person breathes properly.

Good breathing is defined as being regular, deep, and slow. It supplies oxygen to the bloodstream, which is vital for the functioning of all bodily organs, especially the heart and brain.

The scriptures tell us that God breathes His life into us physically and spiritually. Jesus breathed upon His disciples to impart the Holy Spirit to them (John 20:22). The early church experienced the Holy Spirit as a rushing mighty wind—a manifestation of the breath of God (Acts 2:1-2).

Today an awareness of the Spirit of God working in our personal lives is often experienced as a "breath of fresh air," one that cleanses and revives us in every part of our being. We need a "breather" in the Lord's presence so that He can even out the rhythm of our lives. Our spirits will be deeply refreshed and renewed.

Pause to receive from the Lord, and see if you don't find yourself slowing down and releasing the tensions of fear, frustration, and futility. You will be able to think more clearly, God's love will flow more freely, and creative ideas will begin to fill your mind. Inhale deeply of His goodness, strength, and love.

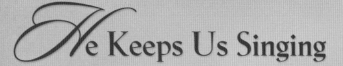e Keeps Us Singing

Evangelist and singer N.B. Vandall was quietly reading his newspaper when one of his sons rushed up to him crying, "Paul is hurt! A car hit him and dragged him down the street! He was bleeding all over, and somebody came and took him away."

Vandall found his son at a nearby hospital with serious head injuries, a concussion, and multiple broken bones. It looked hopeless. All the distraught father could do was pray as the doctors tried to save the boy's life. The rest was up to God.

A peace that passes understanding seemed to fall over Vandall after he went home to pray. He went to the piano and in minutes wrote a hymn entitled "After."

> *After the toil and the heat of the day,*
> *After my troubles are past,*
> *After the sorrows are taken away,*
> *I shall see Jesus at last.*
> *He will be waiting for me—*
> *Jesus so kind and true;*
> *On His beautiful throne,*
> *He will welcome me home—*
> *After the day is through.*

Paul had a near perfect recovery from his injuries, and his father's faith in God remained strong and steady, his gratitude boundless.[1]

God wants to be with you in the midst of your troubles too, putting a song of praise in your mouth. Turn your focus from your struggles to Him. His awesome power can overcome whatever you are facing.

HE PUT A NEW SONG IN MY MOUTH,

A SONG OF PRAISE TO OUR GOD.

MANY WILL SEE AND FEAR,

AND PUT THEIR TRUST IN THE LORD.

PSALM 40:3 NRSV

IT IS GOD WHO ARMS ME
WITH STRENGTH
AND MAKES MY WAY PERFECT.

2 SAMUEL 22:33 NIV

Straight Ahead

The annoying alarm clock blares in your ear, and you groggily reach over to fumble with the snooze button. *Just a few more minutes,* you think, *and then I can get up and face the day.* The alarm sounds again. You know you can't put it off any longer. It's time to face the inevitable. It's time to wrestle another day to the ground. But first, seek inspiration from this prayer written by Jacob Boehme, a German shoemaker who lived more than four hundred years ago:

Rule over me this day, O God, leading me on the path of righteousness. Put Your Word in my mind and Your truth in my heart, that this day I neither think nor feel anything except what is good and honest. Protect me from all lies and falsehood, helping me to discern deception wherever I meet it. Let my eyes always look straight ahead on the road You wish me to tread, that I might not be tempted by any distraction. And make my eyes pure, that no false desires may be awakened within me.[2]

Approaching life prayerfully can help you have the following:

- a day without distractions, focused only on the important
- a day viewed through pure eyes
- a day marked by goodness and honesty
- a day of clear direction and no deception
- a day without falsehood and lies
- a day in which God's Word rules your mind and His truth reigns in your heart

"DO NOT LET YOUR LEFT HAND KNOW
WHAT YOUR RIGHT HAND IS DOING, SO THAT
YOUR GIVING MAY BE IN SECRET.
THEN YOUR FATHER, WHO SEES WHAT IS DONE
IN SECRET, WILL REWARD YOU."

MATTHEW 6: 3–4 NIV

Spontaneous Love Bouquets

Melanie read the suggestions carefully. "Place contrasting colors together, like peach with blue. Or try red, white, and blue for a bright, patriotic bed. If you prefer, naturalize your bulbs, incorporating them into your yard's natural habitat. This works particularly well if you live in a wooded, grassy area."

She grabbed her gardener's tools and set to work, planting some in circles and others in rows. Melanie reserved a handful of varied-size bulbs, and like a mother hiding Easter eggs for her child, she tossed bulbs randomly onto the grass. Wherever they landed, Melanie carved a hole and dropped them into the ground.

One early spring day, Melanie walked out into her backyard and saw green shoots poking through the earth. In the next few weeks, her yard looked like a magical wonderland. It was fun to see the bulbs pop up among the natural setting—beside trees, in the middle of a grassy slope, or tucked away in a corner. Melanie's long-forgotten efforts were rewarded with a harvest of beautiful flowers.

Christlike deeds resemble Melanie's garden. Some we plant in deliberate, orderly fashion. Others spill out from our lives naturally, like spontaneous love bouquets to those around us.

ightrope Trust

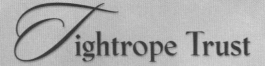

In the mid-nineteenth century, tightrope walker Blondin stretched a two-inch steel cable across Niagara Falls. A large crowd gathered to watch, and he asked them, "Do you believe that I can carry the weight of a man on my shoulders across this gorge?"

They shouted and cheered, and Blondin carried a 180-pound sack of sand across the cable. Then Blondin asked, "Do you believe I can actually carry a person across the gorge?" Again the crowd cheered him on.

"Which one of you will climb on my shoulders and let me carry you across the falls?" Silence fell across the crowd. Everyone wanted to see this feat, but nobody wanted to put his or her life into Blondin's hands.

Finally he had a volunteer for this death-defying stunt: his manager, who had known Blondin for many years. As they prepared to cross the falls, Blondin instructed his manager, "You must not trust your own feelings, but mine. You will feel like turning when we don't need to turn. And if you trust your feelings, we will both fall. You must become part of me." The two made it across to the other side safely.[3]

Jesus gives us the same instruction when we are asked to trust Him in difficult circumstances: "Don't trust your own feelings, trust Me to carry you through."

I KNOW WHOM I HAVE BELIEVED,
AND AM PERSUADED THAT HE IS ABLE
TO KEEP THAT WHICH I HAVE COMMITTED
UNTO HIM AGAINST THAT DAY.

2 TIMOTHY 1:12

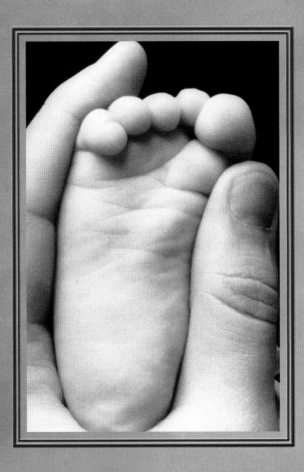

I WILL PRAISE THEE;

FOR I AM FEARFULLY *AND* WONDERFULLY MADE:

MARVELLOUS *ARE* THY WORKS;

AND *THAT* MY SOUL KNOWETH RIGHT WELL.

PSALM 139:14

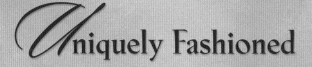

Uniquely Fashioned

When you stop to think about all the intricate details involved in the normal functioning of your body—just one creation among countless species and organisms on the planet—you must conclude, "The Designer of *this* piece of work had a marvelous plan."

Listen to your heartbeat. Flex your fingers and toes. Remember the following:

- No one else among all humanity has your exact fingerprints, handprints, or footprints.

- No one else has your voiceprint.

- No one else has your genetic code—the exact positioning of the many genes that define your physical characteristics.

Furthermore, nobody else has your exact history in time and space. Nobody else has gone where you've gone, done what you've done, said what you've said, or created what you've created. You are truly a one-of-a-kind masterpiece.

The Lord knows precisely *how* you were made and *why* you were made. When something in your life goes amiss, He knows how to fix it. When you err or stray from His commandments, He knows how to woo you back.

You have been uniquely fashioned for a specific purpose on the earth. He has a "design" for your life. It is His own imprint, His own mark.

Worry Wednesday

Do you ever worry if you made a right decision yesterday or did the wrong thing tonight or what tomorrow holds? One woman decided to set aside one day each week to worry. As difficult situations occurred, she would write them down and put them in her worry box. Then, on "Worry Wednesday," she would read them. To her amazement, most of the things had already worked out.

American poet Ellen M. Huntington Gates described God's perfect rest for those with weary hearts in her poem "Sleep Sweet."

> *Sleep sweet within this quiet room,*
> *O thou, whoe'er thou art,*
> *And let no mournful yesterdays*
> *Disturb thy peaceful heart.*
> *Nor let tomorrow mar thy rest*
> *With dreams of coming ill:*
> *Thy Maker is thy changeless friend,*
> *His love surrounds thee still.*
> *Forget thyself and all the world,*
> *Put out each garish light:*
> *The stars are shining overhead*
> *Sleep sweet! Good night! Good night!*[4]

As a child of God, you can rest in the knowledge that you are surrounded by a loving Father who cares for you. The same Creator who placed each star in the sky is watching over you.

"DO NOT WORRY ABOUT TOMORROW,

FOR TOMORROW WILL

WORRY ABOUT ITS OWN THINGS.

SUFFICIENT FOR THE DAY IS ITS OWN TROUBLE."

MATTHEW 6:34 NKJV

THE CITY HAS NO NEED OF THE SUN
NOR OF THE MOON TO GIVE LIGHT TO IT,
FOR THE SPLENDOR *AND*
RADIANCE (GLORY) OF GOD ILLUMINATE IT,
AND THE LAMB IS ITS LAMP.

REVELATION 21:23 AMP

Soul Hunger

One spring, despite endless cloudy days, the columbines still managed to bloom. Blue, scarlet, and gold bell-shaped flowers with delicate dangling spurs towered over lacy foliage. They danced gracefully in the breeze, their bright colors attracting hummingbirds. Yet, without God's sun, they didn't seem as radiant as in previous springs.

It is the same with humans. Although we follow our genetic codes and grow into healthy people physically, we have no radiance without the Son of God. The windows of our souls appear cloudy, and God's love cannot shine through us.

Just as columbines hunger for the sun's warm rays, our souls hunger for the loving presence of Jesus. Unlike the columbines, however, we can find the Son even on cloudy days of despair. Getting to know Him in a personal way enlightens our souls. His radiance fills our hearts and enlivens our spirits with hope for eternal life with Him in Heaven.

In Heaven the sun will not be needed because God himself will be our light. Perhaps Heaven's columbines will always dance with radiance from the glow of God's glory.

"TAKE MY YOKE UPON YOU AND LEARN
FROM ME, FOR I AM GENTLE
AND HUMBLE IN HEART, AND YOU WILL
FIND REST FOR YOUR SOULS."

MATTHEW 11:29 NIV

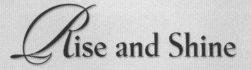

Rise and Shine

Janie jolted awake at the sound of her alarm clock. She was not at all sure why she went to the trouble. It seemed especially vague and worthless the moments before her head settled back down onto the pillow.

"No!" she yelled at herself, waking up again with a start. She had promised God she would awake early for a morning devotional time, even if she went around for the rest of the day with a sleep-deprived, grumpy attitude. She took out her Bible, her notebook, and a devotional. Her attitude brightened.

Once she was up, every moment was worth it. Meeting God in the early morning hours didn't make her grumpy as she always anticipated, but instead she felt revitalized and peaceful. The early morning moments gave her a chance to see the sunrise, to watch an occasional bird, to enjoy the silence of a world not yet awake. It took awhile to convince her body of the benefits of such early rising, but soon it became habit. After awhile, the only time she experienced grumpiness was when she missed her morning meeting with God.

Taking the time with our Savior in the early morning hours is better than fine cappuccino and the smell of omelettes and bacon. It is the best part of the day.

Working Together

Toyohiko Kagawa was a noted Japanese poet and Christian social reformer. Although he suffered poor health, he lived among the needy in the slums and worked tirelessly to overcome social injustice. His poem "Work" speaks of the source of his strength:

The troubled people
Should expect to be
Busy always.
Christ was so thronged
By multitudes
He had no time to eat.
He said,
"To him that hath
Shall be given;
And from him that hath not
Shall be taken away
Even that
He seems to have."
Which means
That if we do not use
All of our powers
We lose them. . . .
Then, too, the problem is
To do our work
With all our hearts;
We do not tire
Of doing what we love.
But most of all,
Our strength and comfort come
Only when God
Dwells in our souls
Working together with us. [5]

No matter what work you do today, you will work with purpose and strength if God is your Partner. He is always with you, waiting for you to simply ask for His strength to finish the job!

As God's partners we beg you
not to toss aside this marvelous message
of God's great kindness.

2 CORINTHIANS 6:1 TLB

I CONSIDER THY HEAVENS,
THE WORK OF THY FINGERS,
THE MOON AND THE STARS,
WHICH THOU HAST ORDAINED.

PSALM 8:3 NASB

The Night Sky

Jamie Buckingham once wrote about taking a night stroll up a mountain in North Carolina:

I wondered about the time, but to glance at my watch would have been sacrilegious. Clocks, calendars, automobiles, and airplanes—instruments of time and speed—were all buried beneath nature's cloak of stillness and slowness. I kicked the snow off my boot, and standing in the middle of the road, threw my head back and breathed deeply of the pine-scented air. Looking into the heavens I could see stars whose light had left there a million years ago, and realized I was just glimpsing the edge of space. Beyond that was infinity—and surrounding it all, the Creator.

I remembered a quote from the German philosopher, Kant. Something about two irrefutable evidences of the existence of God: the moral law within and the starry universe above. I breathed His name: "God."

Then, overwhelmed by His presence, I called Him what I had learned to call Him through experience: "Father!" [6]

Tonight, contemplate the stars in the heavens. You will find there a glimpse of eternity. What an awesome thought: *The Creator of the universe invites you to have a personal relationship with Him!*

What Shape Are You In?

In ancient societies clay pots were valuable tools. Large jars stored olive oil, grain, and other foods. Jugs held water, and small terra-cotta vials contained perfume. Families used clay pots and bowls for cooking and eating. Homes were lit by clay lamps.

The potters who supplied these much-needed vessels were important to the economic life of ancient villages. A modern potter described her craft like this:

Both my hands shaped this pot. The place where it actually forms is a place of tension between the pressure applied from the outside and the pressure of the hand on the inside. That's the way my life has been. Sadness and death and misfortune and the love of friends influenced my life. But the things I believe in about myself, my faith in God and the love of some friends worked on the inside of me. My life, like this pot, is the result of what happened on the outside and what was going on inside me.[7]

Throughout the day we may be buffeted by stress, pulled apart by responsibilities, and pressed by challenges that come at us from the outside. Without God helping us inside, those difficulties can cause our "vessels" to collapse under the external pressure. Your inner life gives you the strength you need to become a useful vessel in the household of God.

THE INWARD *MAN* IS BEING

RENEWED DAY BY DAY.

2 CORINTHIANS 4:16 NKJV

DO NOT FORGET TO ENTERTAIN
STRANGERS, FOR BY SO DOING
SOME PEOPLE HAVE ENTERTAINED ANGELS
WITHOUT KNOWING IT.

HEBREWS 13:2 NIV

An Angel in Deed

The hospital room was quiet as Natalie contemplated her operation scheduled for the next day. She was new in town and felt alone, which was adding to her fear. Sleep would not come, and the night dragged along. The quietness of the room closed in on her.

She was ready to cry when she heard the creaking of the door. "Hi," a woman with a kind face said. "Are you lonely?"

"I sure am," Natalie replied.

"I'm a nursing student. I've caught up on all my paperwork. Do you feel like talking?" she asked.

"I sure do," Natalie replied gratefully. The compassion in the student's eyes comforted Natalie as their conversation soon turned to God and His amazing grace. Slowly, the heavy burden of fear in Natalie's heart began to lift. After a couple of hours, she finally drifted off to sleep, and the student quietly left the room. The next morning, Natalie asked about the student nurse, but no one on the new shift had a clue as to her identity.

What had started out as one of the darkest nights of her life ended in peaceful contentment and sweet dreams, thanks to a young person with a kind heart. Whether the student was a celestial angel or an earthly angel of mercy, she was an angel in deed. She brought peace to Natalie's heart and joy to her soul. Isn't that what God sends His angels to do?

Morning Praise!

A young career woman moved to New York City and rented a room from an elderly Swedish lady who offered a clean room, a shared bathroom, and use of the kitchen at a reasonable rate.

The little white-haired Swedish woman made the rules of the house very clear. There would be no smoking or drinking, no food in the bedrooms, etc. Pausing mid-sentence, the landlady asked, "Do you sing? Do you play? Music is good! I used to play the piano but not now. I'm too old. My hearing isn't good, but I love to praise God with music. God loves music."

After a full day of moving into her new room, the young tenant slept soundly until 5:30 A.M. when she was jarred awake by horrible noises coming from somewhere downstairs. Cautiously making her way down the stairway, she followed the sounds to the kitchen door. There she discovered her new landlady standing at the stove, dressed for the day, joyfully "singing" at the top of her lungs! Never had the young woman heard such a horrible voice. Yet she heard that voice, precious to God, start every morning off the same way for as long as she rented the room.

The tenant moved on, married, and had her own family. She is alone now also and has lost some of her hearing. Yet every morning finds her standing in front of the stove, singing off key her loud—but joyful—praises to the Lord!

COME BEFORE HIM

WITH JOYFUL SINGING.

PSALM 100:2 NASB

God is light and in him is no darkness at all.

1 John 1:5

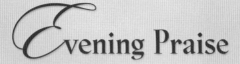

Evening Praise

The Book of Common Prayer has a hymn called "Phos Hilaraon" or "O Gracious Light":

O gracious Light,
pure brightness of the everliving Father in heaven,
O Jesus Christ, holy and blessed!
Now as we come to the setting of the sun,
and our eyes behold the vesper light,
we sing your praises, O God:
Father, Son, and Holy Spirit.
You are worthy at all times to be praised
by happy voices,
O Son of God, O Giver of life,
and to be glorified through all the worlds.

God's light never leaves us. He is with us always, day and night. Ancient pagans believed that night was a time of death and sadness, a time of a "departure of the gods" from the world. This hymn proclaims the exact opposite. Jesus Christ gives life around the clock. The Father never abandons His children, and He is worthy of praise at all times.

In the book of Revelation, John describes the New Jerusalem, our eternal home, with these words:

There shall be no night there; and they need no candle,
neither light of the sun; for the Lord God giveth them light:
and they shall reign for ever and ever.
Revelation 22:5

Scientists today tell us that if anything is reduced to its purest form of energy, it becomes light and heat—the sun in miniature. The Gospel tells us the Son of God is our unending supply of energy and life.

[JESUS] SAID TO THEM,

"COME WITH ME BY YOURSELVES

TO A QUIET PLACE

AND GET SOME REST."

MARK 6:31 NIV

 Scheduled Rest

Schedules. Sometimes we feel as though we're governed by to-do lists. The calendar overflows with notations: do this, go here, pick that up, buy this, deliver that, or mail this other thing. And just when we think we're on top of our lives, someone adds a new item to our to-do list.

Stress. Americans are plagued with stress-related health problems like heart disease, high blood pressure, bad cholesterol, and arthritis.

How can we keep the daily pressures of life from becoming debilitating stress? God's solution has always been to take a day of rest. Return to the simple pleasures. Conversation used to be the primary form of entertainment—not the television, radio, or CD player. Comforting aromas wafting from the kitchen greeted family members throughout the day.

Toss out the bottle of aspirin and put your daily planner away for one day each week. Make sure everyone in the family knows that this will be a "scheduled" day of rest. Before you go to bed the night before, use your modern appliances to help give you a jump start on the day. Pop some dough ingredients into the bread machine and set the timer on the coffeepot. You'll awaken to the smell of freshly perked coffee and freshly baked bread. Those inviting aromas will make you want to savor your scheduled rest time with your family.

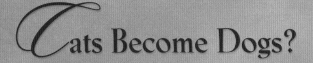Cats Become Dogs?

It had been years since the four siblings had been together, and the air was filled with laughter as they regaled their families with stories from their childhood. The three older brothers told story after story of the trials and tribulations of having three boys in one bedroom. They also told of the many practical jokes they had played on one another and of the numerous fights they had had as kids. But no one could top Sherry's story of being the "baby sister."

"You know, guys," she said during a momentary lull in the conversation, "I used to think that all cats would one day turn into dogs and that all people were born girls and would eventually turn into boys. In fact, I used to wonder when I would become a boy just like you guys."

When she was just a child, Sherry's concept made perfect sense. Of course, as she grew old enough to understand things better, this idea slipped away to become just a fond memory.

While physical growth and maturation occur independent of our control, how many times do we remain "children in our understanding" because we simply choose *not* to exercise our thinking abilities, or because the issues we must face are just too uncomfortable? Yet we can seek God's wisdom and direction so that we may grow in our understanding of His desires for us.

Are you willing to accept that challenge today?

BRETHREN, BE NOT CHILDREN

IN UNDERSTANDING.

1 CORINTHIANS 14:20

*N*ever Diet Again

It's you against all those fattening desserts: pies, cookies, cakes, candy. You have declared war on fat. You've carefully read food labels, measured portions, cut out the fatty foods from your diet, and exercised regularly. But did you know there's an easier way to stay healthy and fit, one that doesn't require you to lose weight to accomplish your goals? In fact, God wants all His children to be FAT—spiritually speaking.

Here's how to gain spiritual weight:

F—Be *faithful* to do all that God tells you to do.
A—Be *available* for His use.
T—Be *teachable*.

Being faithful to God means holding on to Him when life's problems are pressing in. You probably would rather run and hide. What if God is transforming you into a stronger person through those trials? Would you still want to run? Being available to God means allowing Him to heal the hidden things deep within your heart—disappointments, hurts, and failings. This will free you to help others, and you will replace old habits with good ones by seeking God's plan for your life. Being teachable means never skimping on your daily nourishment from the Bible. Feed your spirit on God's Word every day, and you won't feel spiritually hungry or deprived.

Go ahead—get FAT with God!

He that putteth his trust
in the Lord shall be made fat.

PROVERBS 28:25

n the Garden

The Garden of Gethsemane was a place of rest—a sanctuary for those who were weary. But its beauty brought Jesus no peace or tranquility as He prayed before His crucifixion. On worn knees He cried out in despair over what would come. The intensity of His agonizing prayer forced droplets of blood through his skin. Facing sure death by crucifixion, He asked of His Heavenly Father, "Must it come to this?" But in the hour of decision, He prayed, "Nevertheless, not My will but Thine be done."

It's comforting to know that if we dread anything, our Lord knows exactly how we feel. He knows what it's like to make sacrifices for loved ones. He knows what it's like to be falsely accused. Our Father knows what it's like to lose someone you love.

We have His assurance that He is always with us. He will never leave us nor forsake us. For a hope in the heavenly life to come for us, He was willing to be the final sacrifice.

Despite His agony, the true end of His story is a happy one. Yes, He suffered and died. But He was resurrected. His triumph is an empty tomb. Whatever you're facing, know that God is walking through it with you. Lean on Him.

I RECKON THAT THE SUFFERINGS
OF THIS PRESENT TIME *ARE* NOT WORTHY
TO BE COMPARED WITH THE GLORY
WHICH SHALL BE REVEALED IN US.

ROMANS 8:18

"TRULY I TELL YOU, WHOEVER DOES
NOT RECEIVE THE KINGDOM OF GOD AS A LITTLE
CHILD WILL NEVER ENTER IT."

MARK 10:15 NRSV

The Scent of Love

Anne was visiting her mother when the temperature took an unexpected drop. She borrowed one of her mother's jackets when she had to go pick up her four-year-old son, Jacob, at preschool.

He immediately commented on what he thought was Anne's "new" jacket, and she said she had borrowed it from his grandmother. He hugged her and exclaimed, "Oh, Mom! It smells!" She was puzzled. Did the jacket smell bad?

Jacob replied, "No, Mommy. It smells good—just like Grandma does!"

The next day Anne told her mother what Jacob had said, not realizing the impact her words had. To have a child identify you by smell evokes a personal and precious feeling; Jacob's sensory recognition made his grandmother feel loved in a very special way.

Babies learn to recognize the sight of their parents' faces and the sounds of their voices. The sense of smell is much more subtle, but it's not unusual for children—and even adults—to experience strong responses to the scents associated with their loved ones.

God wants us to know Him so well that we can recognize Him. While our Lord is not Someone we can actually see or hear or smell with our natural senses, our spirits can recognize the sweet "aroma" of Him caring for us, blessing us, and surrounding us with His love.

THE PRIDE OF THINE HEART HATH DECEIVED THEE,

THOU THAT DWELLEST IN THE CLEFTS

OF THE ROCK, WHOSE HABITATION *IS* HIGH;

THAT SAITH IN HIS HEART,

WHO SHALL BRING ME DOWN TO THE GROUND?

OBADIAH 1:3

Faulty Assumptions

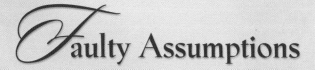

A traveler at an airport bought a small package of cookies to eat while reading a newspaper. Gradually, she became aware of a rustling noise. Looking from behind her paper, she was flabbergasted to see the man sitting beside her help himself to the cookies on the table. Not wanting to make a scene, she leaned over and took a cookie herself.

A minute later, she heard more rustling. He was helping himself to another cookie! She was angry but didn't dare allow herself to say anything. As if to add insult to injury, the man broke the last cookie in two, pushed half across to her, ate the other half, and left.

Still fuming later when her flight was announced, the woman opened her handbag to get her ticket. To her shock and embarrassment, there was her pack of unopened cookies!

Pride caused the woman in this story to make the faulty assumption that she was right and the gentleman was wrong. Instead of seeing him through God's eyes and praying for wisdom to handle the situation God's way, she was completely blind to his kindness toward her.

When you find yourself in a conflict with others, avoid prideful assumptions by walking in God's love. See other people and situations through His eyes. After all, your vision is limited, but He knows exactly what's going on!

Lasting Legacies

Marian Wright Edelman, attorney and founding president of the Children's Defense Fund, often speaks of how Martin Luther King had a profound impact on her life. All Americans have been affected by Dr. King's life in some way, and few have not heard his famous comment, "I have a dream." But it was not his public persona that impacted her; it was his willingness to admit his fears.

She writes, "I remember him as someone able to admit how often he was afraid and unsure about his next step. It was his human vulnerability and his ability to rise above it that I most remember."

Ms. Edelman knew about rising above fear and uncertainty. She grew up during the days of segregation, one of five children, the daughter of a Baptist minister. She graduated from Spelman College and Yale University Law School and was the first black woman to pass the bar in the state of Mississippi. She is a prolific writer who has devoted her life to serving as an activist for disadvantaged Americans, especially children.

Hers is an incredible testimony to the belief in helping others to help themselves. "I have always believed that I could help change the world because I have been lucky to have adults around me who did—in small and large ways."

We have the same opportunity. Will we respond as well as she? Will we help change the world?

GOOD WILL COME TO HIM
WHO IS GENEROUS AND LENDS FREELY,
WHO CONDUCTS HIS AFFAIRS
WITH JUSTICE.

PSALM 112:5 NIV

Grow Up!

"Grow up!" is a taunt often used toward people who aren't acting as mature as they should at the moment. The command is given with the attitude that the other person can simply make a choice to immediately grow up.

Commanding someone to grow up doesn't do any more good than it would to tell a tree to grow up. The growing process takes time—lots of it. Every living thing requires certain elements in order to grow—good soil, the appropriate amounts of sunshine and water, and plenty of time.

People, like trees, need a good start in order to be rooted securely. Young saplings can't mature into tall, beautiful shade trees without the right mixture of sun, water, rich soil, and space. As long as a tree is living, it never stops growing and never outgrows its need for nourishment.

In God's perfect timing, we do indeed grow up. The growth process is a long one, and it never really is complete. Flourishing trees don't strain to grow. They merely follow the natural process God planted in them. And healthy trees don't decide to just ignore the nourishment of sun, rain, and soil. Instead, they continually draw life from these things.

No matter what our season of life, growing up is a continual process—and it all happens in God's time.

HE WILL BE LIKE

A TREE FIRMLY PLANTED BY

STREAMS OF WATER,

WHICH YIELDS ITS FRUIT

IN ITS SEASON.

PSALM 1:3 NASB

BELOVED, WHATEVER IS TRUE,
WHATEVER IS HONORABLE, WHATEVER IS JUST,
WHATEVER IS PURE, WHATEVER IS PLEASING,
WHATEVER IS COMMENDABLE, IF THERE IS ANY
EXCELLENCE AND IF THERE IS ANYTHING WORTHY
OF PRAISE, THINK ABOUT THESE THINGS.

PHILIPPIANS 4:8 NRSV

Pillars of Stone

Hidden beneath the Chihuahuan Desert in New Mexico lies one of God's great wonders, Carlsbad Caverns. Within its subtle grandeur, tiny drops of water have built a startlingly beautiful monument forty feet high. Drop after drop deposited particle after particle until a marble-like finger grew.

A similar process goes on inside each of us. As a single thought finds its way into our mind, it leaves sediment that sinks deep down within our soul, forming our own pillars—pillars of character. If we let immoral, selfish, and violent thoughts fill our minds, we form eroding pillars of evil and failure. If we fill our minds with truth and love, we form strong and beautiful pillars within our souls.

In Proverbs 23:7, King Solomon said, *As he thinketh in his heart, so is he.* Solomon understood that the things we dwell on determine the people we become. When we pursue God, we begin to reflect His character in our lives. Just as the Carlsbad Caverns were developed over time, hidden from view, so our own true character is built.

INCLINE YOUR EAR TO WISDOM,

AND APPLY YOUR HEART TO UNDERSTANDING.

PROVERBS 2:2 NKJV

Get Understanding

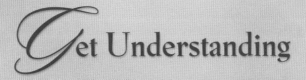

Sometimes it seems life is lived backwards! When we are young with a limited perspective, we have to make the huge decisions that will shape the rest of our lives. But we can—and are wise to—learn from those who have gained insight from experience.

In a study, fifty people over the age of ninety-five were asked the question: If you could live your life over again, what would you do differently? Three general responses emerged from the questionnaire:

- I would reflect more.
- I would risk more.
- I would do more things that would live on after I am dead.[9]

An elderly woman once wrote: "I'd make more mistakes next time; I'd relax; I would limber up; I would be sillier than I have been this trip; I would take fewer things seriously; I would take more chances; I would climb more mountains and swim more rivers; I would eat more ice cream and less beans; I would perhaps have more actual troubles, but I'd have fewer imaginary ones."

Listen and learn! Life cannot be all work and no play, and yet you want your life to be meaningful, to God, to your loved ones who follow you, and to yourself. Reflect on your life. Ask God to show you the true meaning of your existence, what you are to accomplish—and how to have fun along the way!

Ruminating on God's Word

Have you ever watched the news before going to bed… and then dreamed about one of the news stories from the broadcast? The last thing we think about just before we doze off settles deep within our subconscious minds. Like clothes twirling in a dryer, thoughts spin around our minds all night and sometimes return as our first thoughts upon awakening.

King David said in Psalm 4:4, *Meditate within your heart on your bed, and be still* (NKJV). Before you fall asleep, think about God's Word and what God is doing in your life. Ask yourself, *What is the condition of my spirit? Am I fulfilling God's plan for my life?* This will deepen your relationship with God and expand your knowledge of Him.

Meditate—or ruminate—on God's Word as you rest. "Ruminate" means to slowly go over in the mind repeatedly. By spending time going over and over a scripture, you can draw from it the depth of its meaning. The Bible reminds us to be transformed by the renewing of the mind.

So before retiring for the night, read some scripture. As you drift off to sleep, meditate on it. When you wake, you will have "ruminated" all night on God's Word, waking refreshed and renewed.

THIS BOOK OF THE LAW SHALL NOT

DEPART FROM YOUR MOUTH,

BUT YOU SHALL MEDITATE IN IT DAY AND NIGHT,

THAT YOU MAY OBSERVE TO DO

ACCORDING TO ALL THAT IS WRITTEN IN IT.

JOSHUA 1:8 NKJV

"THE SON SAID UNTO HIM,
FATHER, I . . . AM NO MORE WORTHY
TO BE CALLED THY SON."

LUKE 15:21

The Invitation

Rita stood on the sidewalk, peering wistfully into the beautiful home. Through the curtained windows were nicely dressed people, chatting with one another and enjoying refreshments. In her hand she clutched an engraved, personal invitation to the dinner party. She had been invited to attend this evening's affair by her professor, who was impressed with her academic abilities and wanted her to meet others at the university.

She carefully fingered the invitation, looked down at her dress that seemed so dull and ordinary in comparison to the gowns she saw through the window, and with sadness turned and slowly walked away.

This poignant and painful scene from the movie *Educating Rita* demonstrates how difficult it is for one to accept the possibility of a new life. Rita came from a lower middle-class family where no one had attended college. She struggled with feelings of inadequacy and was forever wondering how she would fit in.

However, thanks to a persistent professor, who saw more in her than she saw in herself, she eventually accepted his invitation to join a new world. By the movie's end, this once modest woman excelled as a scholar.

The invitation to become and then excel as a Christian is for each of us. The greatest joy, though, is in knowing that our Teacher always sees much more in us than we usually see in ourselves.

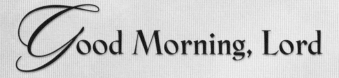

Good Morning, Lord

There is something extraordinarily special about early morning devotions. Before the hectic day begins with its noise and numerous distractions, there is usually a calm that is uncommon to any other time of the day, a calm that is a peaceful prerequisite for entering into the prayer closet with Christ.

Prayer can be a wonderfully private time, where intimate conversation and gentle responses can take place between God and His children. This is a time to listen to the very heart of God.

Oswald Chambers said, "Get an inner chamber in which to pray where no one knows you are praying, shut the door and talk to God in secret. Have no other motive than to know your Father in Heaven. It is impossible to conduct your life as a disciple without definite times of secret prayer."

Between Midnight and Morning
You that have faith to look with fearless eyes
Beyond the tragedy of a world of strife,
And trust that out of night and death shall rise
The dawn of ampler life;
Rejoice, whatever anguish rend your heart,
That God has given you, for a priceless dower,
To live in these great times and have your part
In Freedom's crowning hour'
That we may tell your sons who see the light
High in heaven—their heritage to take—
"I saw the powers of darkness put to flight!
I saw the morning break!"
—Owen Seaman

In the morning, O Lord,
Thou wilt hear my voice; In the
morning I will order *my prayer*
to Thee and *eagerly* watch.

Psalm 5:3 NASB

HE TENDS HIS FLOCK LIKE A SHEPHERD:

HE GATHERS THE LAMBS IN HIS ARMS AND

CARRIES THEM CLOSE TO HIS HEART;

HE GENTLY LEADS THOSE THAT HAVE YOUNG.

ISAIAH 40:11 NIV

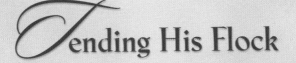

Tending His Flock

Eight-year-old Jonathan was always tempting fate. His mother often held her breath watching him climb to the highest tree branches. Swaying in the breeze, he'd holler, "Hey Mom, watch me!"

One day his mother watched in disbelief as Jonathan rode his bike downhill headed for a swing set minus the swings. At breakneck speed, he stood on the bicycle seat and grabbed the top bar of the swing set. She stifled a scream as he flipped over the top of the bar and landed flat on his back on the cold, hard ground. She ran to his side and carried him home.

Jonathan's chest ached from having the wind knocked out of him. But when his mother called the doctor's office, Jonathan insisted he was fine. She hung up and began checking him for any sign of injury. She was surprised to find ballpoint pen circles around every cut, scrape, and bruise.

"What is all this?" she asked.

"That's all my hurts. I put a circle around all of them," he said. Within minutes, he'd forgotten his pain, wolfed down a bowl of mint chocolate-chip ice cream, and ran back outside.

Like a loving mother, God gathers His children up in His arms time and again, carrying them close to His heart. We may never know how many times God's providential hand has prevented an injury, either physical or emotional, in our lives. Our Shepherd watches over us.

Living Water

Horticulturists tell us that plants thrive on slow, deep watering to a depth of four to six inches. When dry weather hits, the plants are more likely to survive, even if they receive water only once a week. Also, watering in the evening hours decreases the evaporation factor that steals moisture from the plants. One thing is certain, healthy plants that produce lush foliage and beautiful fruit or flowers demand plenty of water carefully applied to their roots. Plant experts say the occasional sprinkling here and there seems to do more damage than good.

Just as plants get thirsty, we get thirsty too. When the Samaritan woman at the well met Jesus, He explained to her that physical water is temporary, but spiritual water is eternal (John 4:13-14). To bear fruit, we need the living water of Christ dwelling within us. If we're always in a hurry and just read a Bible verse here and there, our roots remain shallow and can wither in dry seasons. Through more extended times alone with God in prayer and in reading His Word, we develop inner nourishment.

When we let God put His living water in our hearts, not only does He satisfy our thirst, He helps us to grow so we can be a nourishing fountain to others.

"IF ANY MAN IS THIRSTY, LET HIM COME TO ME
AND DRINK. HE WHO BELIEVES IN ME,
AS THE SCRIPTURE SAID, 'FROM HIS INNERMOST
BEING SHALL FLOW RIVERS OF LIVING WATER.'"

JOHN 7:37–38 NASB

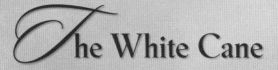he White Cane

The first time Cathi saw Hank, a cantankerous old man, he was waving his white cane and yelling at the top of his lungs. Part of Cathi's job as a caseworker for the state's social services division was to visit elderly residents in their homes.

Hank had been tall and robust before age took its toll on his body. His eighty-year-old body might have shrunk in stature, but his mind was still sharp, and Cathi was just another thorn in his side when she was assigned as his new caseworker.

Cathi struggled with anxiety when it was time to visit Hank, but slowly she began to detect an undercurrent of sadness in the old man. He had outlived his friends and family, including his wife, and he had no children. *Life must be lonely for Hank,* she thought. *Maybe his cane-waving was a bid for attention, the way a two-year-old throws a temper tantrum.*

With time and patience, Cathi earned Hank's trust and respect. She discovered that he was an intelligent man whose body had just gotten too old for him. He simply couldn't do the things he wanted to do, and he was understandably frustrated.

Sometimes we have to be willing to see past people's rough edges and see who they are inside. Do you have a "Hank" in your family or neighborhood? That person may suffer from loneliness, just as Hank did. Will you be a friend?

RISE IN THE PRESENCE OF THE AGED,

SHOW RESPECT FOR THE ELDERLY

AND REVERE YOUR GOD. I AM THE LORD.

LEVITICUS 19:32 NIV

THIS IS THE DAY THE LORD HAS MADE;
WE WILL REJOICE AND BE GLAD IN IT.

PSALM 118:24 NKJV

As Time Goes By

"Where does the time go?" we ask. Last week seems like yesterday, and last year flew by like a video in fast forward.

And worse, it's hard to remember what we spent it on.

Shouldn't I have more great memories? What did I accomplish? Is this all I've done with all that time?

Singer Jim Croce mused in his hit song "Time in a Bottle" that "there never seems to be enough time to do the things you want to do, once you find them." We search for happiness, but happiness is not a goal to be won, but a by-product of a life well spent.

This "Old English Prayer" offers simple instruction for enjoying the day that the Lord has made:

Take time to work, it is the price of success.
Take time to think, it is the source of power.
Take time to play, it is the secret of perpetual youth.
Take time to read, it is the foundation of wisdom.
Take time to be friendly, it is the road to happiness.
Take time to dream, it is hitching your wagon to a star.
Take time to love and be loved, it is the privilege of the gods.
Take time to look around, it is too short a day to be selfish.
Take time to laugh, it is the music of the soul.

SING TO THE LORD A NEW SONG; SING TO THE LORD,
ALL THE EARTH. SING TO THE LORD,
PRAISE HIS NAME; PROCLAIM HIS SALVATION DAY
AFTER DAY. DECLARE HIS GLORY AMONG THE NATIONS,
HIS MARVELOUS DEEDS AMONG ALL PEOPLES.

PSALM 96:1–3 NIV

Larkspur Lives

Pauline planted larkspur seeds and was delighted by their whimsical abundance when they sprouted. When a slight breeze ruffled through them, she was sure she heard tiny giggles of joy because the larkspurs knew God had created their beauty.

The larkspurs' tall flower stalks formed a chorus of pink, blue, white, purple, and occasional splashes of lilac singers. Flowers have the delightful capacity to sing songs for the eyes instead of the ears. This larkspur choir sang a new song of praises that delighted Pauline's soul. The larkspurs stood tall and straight, like vertical musical staffs filled with trills of colored notes all the way up their stalks.

Our Christian walk can be a larkspur life. If we celebrate each new day and count each blessing and share God's love with others, our lives can be a chorus of joyful praise. Like the cheerful larkspur, we can delight those around us. We can be an observable witness of God's marvelous deeds.

Can others hear you singing?

These six *things* doth the Lord hate:
Yea, seven *are* an abomination unto him:
A proud look, a lying tongue, and hands
that shed innocent blood, An heart
that deviseth wicked imaginations, feet
that be swift in running to mischief,
A false witness *that* speaketh lies, and he
that soweth discord among brethren.

PROVERBS 6:16–19

Sugar or Lemon?

Afternoon tea is traditionally a time for reflecting on the day and chatting with friends. Perhaps because it comes at a low-energy time of day, we may be more careless in our conversation and include not-so-kind opinions about others.

At the very time sugar and cream are being slipped into the tea, verbal raspberries, lemons, and sour grapes may slip into the conversation.

But we can choose to make our conversations a time of blessing instead of cursing.

I Know Something Good About You

Wouldn't this world be better, If folks whom we meet would say
"I know something good about you," And treat you just that way?
Wouldn't it be splendid, If each handshake, good and true,
Carried with it this assurance: "I know something good about you?"
Wouldn't life be happier, If the good that's in us all,
Were the only thing about us That people would recall?
Wouldn't our days be sweeter, If we praised the good we see;
For there is a lot of goodness, In the worst of you and me?
Wouldn't it be fine to practice, This way of thinking too;
You know something good about me, I know something good about you?

—Author Unknown

orning People

God made both the day and the night, and He called both of them good. It seems God also made "morning people," who have their greatest energy level in the morning, and "night people," who are most productive in the late hours. If you are a morning person, you are in good company. Scripture is filled with stories about people who rose early to meet God or to be about doing God's will, among them Abraham, Moses, Joshua, Gideon, Job, and even Jesus. The Gospels tell us that Jesus went at dawn to teach the people who gathered in the temple courts.

God promised the children of Israel that they would see the glory

GOD CALLED THE LIGHT DAY, AND THE

of the Lord in the morning (Exodus 16:7 NIV). God supplied manna every morning until they reached the Promised Land. Like the children of Israel, we too can see the glory of the Lord when we seek Him in His Word.

Morning often represents an end to suffering and sadness (Psalm 30:5). Each day brings us a fresh perspective on life. When we give every minute and every circumstance of each day to the Lord, we can expect to see His light dawning throughout our day.

The most glorious event of Christianity—the Resurrection—occurred in the early morning. Each morning we can celebrate Jesus' resurrection as we watch the light of the day dispel the darkness of night.

DARKNESS HE CALLED NIGHT. GENESIS 1:5 NKJV

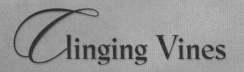
Clinging Vines

Scuppernong vines are parasites that grow up the trunks of, and cling to, healthy, firmly rooted trees in the southern United States. This walnut-sized, dark-skinned wild grape is used to make jams and jellies, and some Southerners use the hull skins for cobbler pies. The fruit produced by these vines has served as an inexpensive treat to poor families in the South for many years. In recent years scuppernongs have become more popular and can be purchased at stores all over the South.

As beautiful, diverse, and tasty as the scuppernong is, it cannot survive on its own. It needs the life support of well-established trees to cling to and draw its nourishment from. Should the scuppernong vine be pulled away from its host tree, it will dry up and stop producing fruit.

Like the scuppernong, we cannot survive without total dependency upon God. Without Him, we have no true life source, no lifeline, no nourishment; and we cannot produce good fruit.

We can, however, learn to cling to the Lord by surrendering ourselves to Him. We can draw nourishment through Bible study, prayer, worship, service, and heartfelt obedience. Like the scuppernong, clinging to our Source will help us grow healthy and produce much good fruit.

"I AM THE VINE, YOU ARE THE BRANCHES;

HE WHO ABIDES IN ME, AND I IN HIM,

HE BEARS MUCH FRUIT;

FOR APART FROM ME YOU CAN DO NOTHING."

JOHN 15:5 NASB

The Sunrise Travelers

When Moses led the Israelites out of Egypt, they experienced great joy upon being delivered from bondage. However, as they crossed the wilderness toward the Promised Land, fear of the unknown would often take hold of their hearts. The following excerpt by Louise Haskins, taken from *Traveling Toward Sunrise,* describes how we all should move into the unknown by simply trusting God:

These travelers were time's valiant great hearts . . . men of faith who followed the gleam loyally, right through to the very end . . . men of vision, always looking ahead, never behind.

What an inspiring, challenging thought as we . . . begin our journey, traveling toward sunrise. . . . we are wayfarers of the infinite, traveling to the land where dawns are begotten and glory has its dwelling place, where life begins, not ends, and where there is eternal springtime.

And I said to the man who stood at the gate of the year, "Give me light that I may tread safely into the unknown!"

And he replied: "Go out into the darkness and put your hand into the Hand of God; That shall be to you better than light and safer than a known way." So I went forth, and finding the Hand of God, trod gladly into the night.[11]

You may be facing tremendous opportunities or overwhelming difficulties. In either case, put your hand into God's hand and walk with Him. Let Him give you comfort and wisdom as you move toward your promised land.

THE CHILDREN OF ISRAEL . . .

JOURNEYED FROM . . .

THE WILDERNESS . . .

TOWARD THE SUNRISING.

NUMBERS 21:10–11

The Still, Small Voice

In his book, *Focus on the Family,* Rolf Zettersten describes his friend, Edwin, who bought a new car. Among the car's features was a recording of a female voice, which gently reminded him to buckle his seat belt or stop for gas.

On one road trip, "the little woman" began informing him that he needed gasoline. "Your fuel level is low," she cooed softly. Edwin thanked her with a smile but decided that he could make it another fifty miles and kept on driving.

Unfortunately, the voice soon warned him again—and again and again until Edwin was ready to scream. Finally he'd had enough. He stopped the car and, after a quick search under the dashboard for the appropriate wires, disconnected the recording. *So much for the little woman,* he thought.

He was still feeling very smug when his car ran out of gas!

God gave us a factory-installed warning voice—the conscience. Sometimes we think it's a nuisance or just plain wrong. However, we learn sooner or later that it's often trying to tell us exactly what we need to know.

Whether you are being told to stop for gas or being warned not to turn off the main road, your conscience knows what is right. Follow it today and see if you don't experience more peace about every decision you make.

My conscience is clear,

BUT THAT DOES NOT MAKE ME INNOCENT.

IT IS THE LORD WHO JUDGES ME.

1 CORINTHIANS 4:4 NIV

As the heavens are higher

than the earth, so are my ways higher

than your ways and my thoughts

than your thoughts.

ISAIAH 55:9 NIV

The Egg Test

Have you ever tried cracking an egg into a bowl while reading a recipe? If you're not adept, you may miss the bowl entirely, and the slippery egg may end up on the floor. Experienced cooks recommend you'll have better success by reading the recipe first, then keeping your eyes on the eggs.

The Bible doesn't discuss eggs and mixing bowls, but it does talk about our focus. When the Israelites first camped on the edge of the Promised Land, God instructed them to do some reconnaissance. Twelve men were sent to look the land over and report back to Moses with their findings. All twelve had seen God miraculously deliver them from slavery and experienced God's provision for their journey. But only two men remembered God and His faithfulness. Only two kept their focus on God; ten men were distracted by the sights and smells of Canaan. Ten men turned their eyes away from God and made a mess for the Israelites that took forty years to clean up.

Whenever we focus on our problems instead of God's promises and possibilities, we're in for a mess. God doesn't view things from our limited perspective. If we want the recipe of our lives to turn out for the best, we need to keep our hearts focused on Him for guidance.

Satisfaction

"Satisfaction guaranteed!" promise the television advertisements. There is no end to the commercial world's promises of fulfilled hopes and dreams.

Do you know many truly satisfied people? Would you describe our culture as satisfied?

We plan and save for years for the "perfect vacation." We head off to our dream-come-true destination, indulge every desire for fun, food, and fantasy; and in two weeks we are headed home with wonderful memories. It may have been a satisfying two weeks, but are we fulfilled for the rest of our lives when the vacation is over?

Perhaps you worked to build the home of your dreams—the place where you are ruler and reign over every affordable luxury and creature comfort. Does it truly satisfy your deepest desires?

In *Mere Christianity*, C.S. Lewis wrote: "If I find in myself a desire which no experience in this world can satisfy, the most probable explanation is that I was made for another world."

We were made for another world—Heaven! The desire for satisfaction is very strong in our lives. However, Scripture tells us there is only one thing that will satisfy: "For in him we live, and move, and have our being; as certain also of your own poets have said, For we are also his offspring" (Acts 17:28).

In Your presence is fullness

of joy.

Psalm 16:11 NKJV

In the morning

my prayer comes before You.

Psalm 88:13 NKJV

irst Cup

Many people wouldn't dream of starting their day without a cup of coffee. They count on that "first cup of the day" to wake them up and get them going.

There are others who have discovered an even more potent day-starter: morning prayer.

For some this is a prayer voiced to God before getting out of bed. For others it is a planned time of prayer between getting dressed and leaving for work. For still others it is a commitment to get to work half an hour early to spend quiet, focused time in prayer before the workday begins.

Henry Ward Beecher, one of the most notable preachers of the nineteenth century, had this to say about starting the day with prayer:

In the morning, prayer is the key that opens to us the treasure of God's mercies and blessings. The first act of the soul in early morning should be a draught at the heavenly fountain. It will sweeten the taste for the day." [12]

Morning prayer is a time to have your cup filled to overflowing with peace. Then as you have contact with other people at home and at work, you can pour that same peace into them. And the good news is— unlimited free refills are readily available anytime your cup becomes empty throughout the day!

The Return on Giving

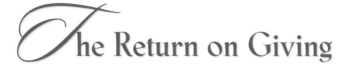

A drowning man gestured frantically to a man standing at the edge of a swimming pool. Splashing his way toward the side of the pool, the drowning man hollered, "Here, let me give you my hand." The man took his hand and pulled the distressed man to safety.

Afterward, the lifesaver said, "I find it unusual that you said, 'Let me give you my hand,' rather than asking me to give you *my* hand."

The rescued man replied, "I work for a charitable organization, sir. I've discovered that people are always more willing to receive than they are to give!"

While our human tendency may be to receive rather than give, the Gospel says that giving is the most productive way to receive! Whatever we extend to others returns to us multiplied. This principle has been recognized by the business community. Donald David has said:

The best basis for being advanced is to organize yourself out of every job you're put in. Most people are advanced because they're pushed up from people underneath them rather than pulled by the top.

Find ways to give to those around you today. Be generous in your praise and encouragement. Give advice on how to do specific tasks more efficiently or with greater quality. The more you do to help others in their work, the easier your own workload will become.

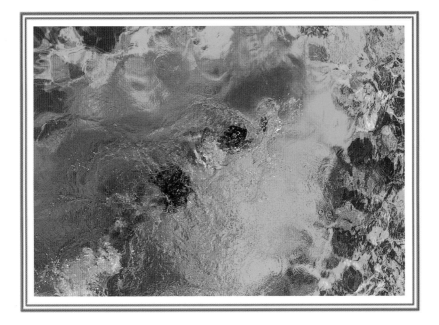

"GIVE, AND IT WILL BE GIVEN TO YOU:
GOOD MEASURE, PRESSED DOWN,
SHAKEN TOGETHER, AND RUNNING OVER."

LUKE 6:38 NKJV

HE LEADETH ME BESIDE THE STILL WATERS.

HE RESTORETH MY SOUL.

PSALM 23:2–3

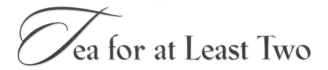ea for at Least Two

The custom of afternoon tea is said to have been created by Anna, duchess of Bedford, in the nineteenth century. At that time the English customarily ate a hearty breakfast, a light lunch at midday, and didn't have dinner until late evening. Understandably hungry long before then, the duchess asked to have a small meal served in her private quarters in the late afternoon. Eventually, she invited close friends to share the repast. While the duchess' initiation of tea-time was aimed at nourishment for her body, she and the rest of England soon discovered that adding beautiful china and good friends to the occasion also nourished the soul.[13]

We are wise to recognize our need for a "spiritual tea-time" each day. Even if we have a "hearty breakfast" in the Word each morning, sometimes the pressures of the day come to bear in late afternoon. Our spirits long for a little peace and refreshment in the presence of our loving Savior, and a quick prayer or the voicing of praise can give our spirits a lift.

Set aside some time in your afternoon to focus on the beauty of life that the Lord has set before you. Create a few moments away from the hustle and bustle of your life before returning to the tasks that await you. Give thanks to the Lord for sharing His presence with you.

Beauty for Ashes

Sharon smiled as she sprayed the glass picture frame with cleaner. The words of the inspirational poem she had written for a friend who was facing cancer surgery came into sharp focus.

The gray December day reminded her of a similar day when she was in seventh grade, and her teacher asked the class to write Christmas poems. Sharon's poem, so different from those of her classmates, was about the birth of the Christ Child. She took it home and rewrote it until the poem shone as the star of Bethlehem itself.

The next day she beamed as her teacher praised her poem and read it to the entire class. Later, however, the teacher asked to speak to her in the hall. There, after talking to another teacher, she accused the child of stealing the poem from a book. Brokenhearted, Sharon wrote no more—until twenty-five years later, when she returned to writing as a form of therapy during troubled times. Only then was her talent realized and later published.

Are you neglecting your talents because someone criticized you in the past? Don't let your gifts become ashes. Whether cooking, serving, speaking, writing, or making something beautiful with your hands, turn them into a crown of beauty for God.

[HE HAS SENT ME] TO BESTOW ON THEM
A CROWN OF BEAUTY INSTEAD OF ASHES,
THE OIL OF GLADNESS INSTEAD
OF MOURNING, AND A GARMENT OF PRAISE
INSTEAD OF A SPIRIT OF DESPAIR.

ISAIAH 61:3 NIV

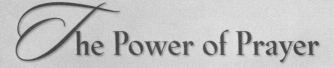The Power of Prayer

Time after time, history has been shaped by prayer.

Queen Mary said she feared the prayers of John Knox more than all the armies of Scotland.

John Wesley's prayers brought revival to England, sparing them the horrors of the French Revolution.

Revival spread throughout the American colonies when Jonathan Edwards prayed.

The Reverend Billy Graham said, "I tell you, history could be altered and changed again if people went to their knees in believing prayer. . . . We have not yet learned that a man can be more powerful on his knees than behind the most powerful weapons that can be developed."[14]

Matthew 14:23 tells us that Jesus sought to be alone with the Father after what must have been an extremely taxing day of preaching, teaching, and healing the multitudes. Perhaps our prayers are *more* powerful when in weariness we drop the pretense of "religious" language in favor of direct communication with the God into whose hands we've placed our lives.

Today, speak honestly and openly with the Lord about your concerns, and make your petitions known. Then cast your cares onto Him and be in peace, knowing He is at work on your behalf.

When he [Jesus] had sent
the multitudes away, he went up into
a mountain apart to pray:
and when the evening was come,
he was there alone.

MATTHEW 14:23

THE STEPS OF A GOOD MAN

ARE ORDERED BY THE LORD.

PSALM 37:25 NKJV

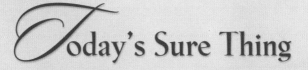

Today's Sure Thing

In his children's book, *The Chance World,* Henry Drummond describes a place in which nothing is predictable. The sun may rise, or it may not. The sun might suddenly appear at any hour, or the moon might rise instead of the sun. If people jump into the air in the "chance world," it is impossible to predict whether they will ever come down again. The fact they came down yesterday is no guarantee that they will come down the next time. Gravity and all the other natural laws change from hour to hour.

In the final analysis, the "chance world" is a frightening world. While most people enjoy a certain amount of spontaneity in their lives, they enjoy life more when it is lived against a backdrop of predictability, surety, and trustworthiness.

The scriptures promise us that the Lord is the same yesterday, today, and forever (Hebrews 13:8). Furthermore, His commandments do not change; His promises to us are *sure* promises. We can know with certainty, "The steps of a good man *are ordered* by the Lord."

The Lord may have some surprises for you today. They are a part of His ongoing creativity in your life. But His surprises are always custom designed for you on the rock-solid foundation of His love. It is always His desire that you experience the highest and best in your life. You can count on Him!

With Attitude

"To love what you do and feel that it matters—how could anything be more fun?" asks Katharine Graham. That's what we all desire, isn't it?

No matter what we do, our work attitude is vital to our basic sense of self-worth. Everyone wants to love the work they do and feel it has significance. While no job is pleasant all the time, it is possible to derive satisfaction from what we bring to a job—the attitude with which we perform our tasks.

Entrepreneurs Ben Cohen and Jerry Greenfield make and sell ice cream with a purpose. The bottom line of Ben & Jerry's Homemade, Inc., is "How much money is left over at the end of the year?" and "How have we improved life in the community?"

"Leftover money" goes to fund Ben & Jerry's Foundation, which distributes funds to worthy nonprofit causes. By helping others with their profits, Ben & Jerry's puts more *meaning* into their ice cream business.

The scriptures say that all service ranks the same with God because it's not *what* you do that matters but the *spirit* in which you do it. A street sweeper who does his work to serve God and bless the travelers on the streets is as pleasing to Him as the priests and pastors who minister to their congregations.

If you feel your work is insignificant, ask God to open your eyes! When you do all for Him and to serve others, no task is unimportant!

Whatever you do,
do all to the glory of God.

1 Corinthians 10:31 RSV

How shall we sing the Lord's song, in a strange land?

Psalm 137:4

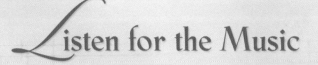

Listen for the Music

George Gershwin was talking to a friend on a crowded beach near New York City when the joyous shrieks of voices pierced their conversation. Clanking tunes ground out from a nearby merry-go-round while barkers and hucksters shouted. Underground was the deep roar of the subway; beside them crashed the relentless waves of the ocean.

Gershwin listened and then remarked to his friend, "All of this could form such a beautiful pattern of sound. It could turn into a magnificent musical piece expressive of every human activity and feeling with pauses, counterpoints, blends, and climaxes of sound that would be beautiful. . . . But it is not that. . . . It is all discordant, terrible, and exhausting—as we hear it now. The pattern is always being shattered."

What a parable of our time! So many confusing noises, so much unrest, so much rapid change. But somewhere in the midst of it, a pattern could emerge; a meaning could come out of it.

Our job is to hear the music in the noise.

Sometimes it takes effort to hear all the tunes around you that make up the symphony of your life. But if you focus on a particular melody, the conflicting chaos swirling around your own symphony will be weeded out as each strain becomes distinguishable. A pattern emerges, and you rejoice in God's unparalleled creativity in His world.

Be a creative listener!

Penny Bear

In the 1950s, one brand of honey came in a glass bottle shaped like a baby bear. Grandma used this brand for cooking and quickly emptied the uniquely shaped container. The honey bottle was too pretty to throw away, so Grandma put it to use as a penny jar. Whenever she came across a penny, it would go into the bear-shaped bottle on her kitchen counter.

Her grandchildren loved to count the pennies in what they called Grandma's "penny bear." Whenever the penny bear was full, Grandma put the pennies into a bank savings account. The empty penny bear reappeared on the kitchen counter, ready for a new collection. The process continued year after year.

When her oldest granddaughter began preparations for college, Grandma said she had something to give her. Entering the kitchen, her granddaughter noticed a piece of paper sticking out of the top of the empty penny bear. It was a check. Because of Grandma's penny-saving habits, there was enough money in the penny-bear account to buy her college textbooks for that first semester and for several more years.

Now whenever her granddaughter finds a penny on the ground, she thanks God for Grandma's faithful stewardship. One penny is not worth much. But one penny multiplied can feed a hungry family, house a homeless person, or help a child through college. Little things *do* mean a lot.

THEY WILL LAY UP TREASURE
FOR THEMSELVES AS A FIRM FOUNDATION
FOR THE COMING AGE.

1 TIMOTHY 6:19 NIV

THERE WAS EVENING,

AND THERE WAS MORNING—

THE FIRST DAY.

GENESIS 1:5 NIV

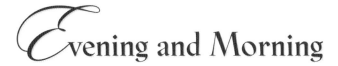

Evening and Morning

In Genesis each day of creation is concluded with the phrase, "and there was evening, and there was morning."

From the Hebrew perspective, so unlike the Western tradition, the day begins at evening, specifically with the setting of the sun. What does it mean for the day to begin at evening?

For Hebrew people through the centuries, the transition from afternoon to evening has been marked by prayer. "Evening prayer" is a Jewish custom. After prayer families gather together for a meal.

The most holy day of the week, the Sabbath, begins with the lighting of candles and a proclamation of faith, then a more formal family dinner. After the evening meal, Jewish families traditionally gather together to read God's Word and discuss how His laws apply to their lives. The evening ends in rest.

It was only after a Hebrew talked with God, enjoyed the love and fellowship of family, studied the Scriptures, and rested that work was undertaken!

What would happen if you adopted this strategy for your evening hours? Would you find yourself more renewed and refreshed, more energetic and healthy, more creative and productive? Might the priorities you desire in your life become a reality?

Why not give it a try? Begin your next day in the evening, and wake up knowing you're totally refreshed—spirit, soul, and body—to have a full and productive day!

The Morning Sacrifice

The Levites never skipped morning devotions. They were commanded to keep the daily morning sacrifice without exception. As part of the morning ritual in the temple, the high priest had three duties:

1. trimming the lamps, to insure the menorah had sufficient oil and that all wicks were properly positioned
2. burning incense on the altar
3. burning the fat of the peace offerings

Once a week the priest also replaced the shewbread that was on constant display before the Lord.

His sacrifices touched upon all aspects of his humanity. The lamps symbolized his need for light—to see with spiritual eyes. The incense expressed his need to dwell in the infusion of God's holy presence. The peace offerings indicated his need for peace with God and his fellow man. And the shewbread demonstrated his need for daily provision, which only the Lord could provide.

This was a ceremony that, in its silence, spoke clearly: "We need You. Without You we have no life, no wholeness, no meaning."

We may not have a ritual to follow in our morning devotional times, but we must come before the Lord with the same spirit of dependency and obedience. The day ahead of us is not ours. Our lives belong to God. (See 1 Corinthians 6:20.)

Everything we need, He will supply. The day is His even as we are His.

THEIR DUTY WAS . . .

TO STAND EVERY MORNING TO THANK

AND PRAISE THE LORD.

1 CHRONICLES 23:28,30 NKJV

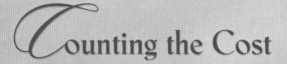 Counting the Cost

Imagine a natural disaster strikes your town, destroying everything in sight. The government predicts it will take ten years to rebuild.

That's what happened to Valmeyer, Illinois, during the 1993 Midwest floods. People who had been neighbors for most of their lives lost everything except their determination to stick together. So they decided to start over and rebuild together—in record time.

To accomplish this monumental task, people had to interrupt their normal lives. After all, there were buildings to construct, funding to secure, and utilities and social services to restore. An entire town had to be rebuilt from scratch.

In this case, a little motivation went far. The $22-million project was completed barely three years after the flood. Helen Keller's statement, "Every day we should do a little more than is required," could have been the motto of the people of Valmeyer. They took that sentiment to heart and rebuilt their town.[15]

Is there something in your life that you could accomplish much sooner by "counting the cost" and then doing a little extra every day, every week, or every month? From paying debts to making health improvements, every project has a momentum that is accelerated when we do "just a little more."

Focus on something important to you, then map out a strategy for an "extra" touch.

"WHICH OF YOU,
INTENDING TO BUILD
A TOWER,
SITTETH NOT DOWN FIRST,
AND COUNTETH
THE COST, WHETHER HE
HAVE *SUFFICIENT*
TO FINISH *IT*?"

LUKE 14:28

The Lord spake unto Moses face to face, as a man speaketh unto his friend.

Exodus 33:11

Quality Time

In his book, *Unto the Hills,* Billy Graham describes a little girl and her father who were great friends. They often went for walks, sharing a passion for watching birds and meeting people who crossed their path.

One day, the father noticed a change in his daughter. If he went for a walk, she excused herself from going. Knowing she was growing up, he rationalized that she must be expected to lose interest in her daddy as she made other friends. Nevertheless, her absence grieved him deeply.

Because of his daughter's absences, he was not in a particularly happy mood on his birthday. Then she presented him with a pair of exquisitely worked slippers, which she had hand made for him while he was on his walks.

At last he understood and said, "My darling, I like these slippers very much, but next time buy the slippers and let me have you all the days. I would rather have my child than anything she can make for me."[16]

Is it possible our heavenly Father sometimes feels lonely for the company of His children? Are we so busy doing good that we forget—or are too weary—to spend some quiet time with Him?

Take a walk with your heavenly Father today. Spend some quality time, talking to Him about anything and everything. You will be blessed, and so will He!

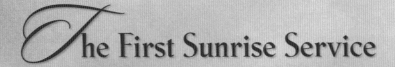

The First Sunrise Service

The year was 1909 at California's Mount Roubidoux. In the valley below the mountain was Mission Inn. Jacob Riis, the famous social crusader and father of slum clearance in New York, was there as a guest.

As Riis looked up at the crest of Mount Roubidoux, he caught a vision. At the inn's evening song service, he shared his thoughts with Frank Miller, the proprietor, and the assembled guests:

I see in the days to come an annual pilgrimage—call it what you will—winding its way up the steps of Mount Roubidoux . . . and gathering there to sing the old songs that go straight to the hearts of men and women.

Riis never dreamed how soon his words would come true. The next Sunday was Easter, and Miller decided to make its observance memorable. He invited one hundred guests and friends to climb Roubidoux, where those one hundred "pilgrims" held the first sunrise service on record.

Today, Easter sunrise services are an annual Christian tradition. While not everyone can celebrate from the top of a mountain, just praising God while watching the first rays of sun appear over the horizon can make one's spirit rise.

There is no need to wait for Easter, however. Why not set your alarm, so you can enjoy your own private "sunrise service" tomorrow morning!

I WILL SING AND GIVE PRAISE.

AWAKE, MY GLORY!

AWAKE, LUTE AND HARP!

I WILL AWAKEN THE DAWN.

PSALM 57:7–8 NKJV

Ask, and it shall be given you;

seek, and ye shall find;

knock, and it shall be opened unto you.

Matthew 7:7

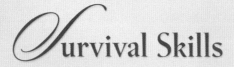urvival Skills

Dressed for office work, Jocelyn didn't look like a person who needed welfare assistance. But so it was. And she was embarrassed to stand in line and pay for her groceries with food stamps. Jocelyn had a job but still didn't have enough money to feed her children, and she felt ashamed.

Earlier she had needed emergency surgery for a rapidly growing ovarian cyst. The doctors feared cancer, while she was more afraid of the hospital bill. But her doctor explained that the welfare system would cover her unexpected expenses.

The same week that Jocelyn needed surgery, her eleven-year-old son was hospitalized with what appeared to be spinal meningitis. The doctors refused to delay her surgery and placed her in a ward without even a telephone. With her son in another hospital miles away, she had never felt so alone. And they were new to the area; there was no one to sit with her young son—not even her.

"Lord, I'm all alone," Jocelyn prayed. "Please help me to talk to my son.

When she told her doctor about her situation, he moved her to a semi-private room where a phone waited beside her bed—all at the doctor's expense.

Are you in desperate need? Put your trust in our loving Father and boldly ask Him for help. He will take care of you.

He knoweth the way that I take:

when he hath tried me,

I shall come forth as gold.

Job 23:10

Under Water

Jewelers claim one of the surest tests of a true diamond is the "underwater test." An imitation diamond is never as brilliant as a genuine stone. If your eye cannot detect the difference, test it by placing the stone under water. The imitation diamond is practically extinguished, while a genuine diamond sparkles, distinctly visible even under water. If a genuine stone is immersed beside an imitation, the contrast will be apparent to even the least experienced eye.

That's how Christians should be when we feel as though we are "under water" at the end of a long day. The power of the Holy Spirit can so sparkle within us (refreshing and renewing us in spite of the day's harassments) that it's easy for others to tell there is something genuinely different about our lives.

Drawing on the power of the Holy Spirit can get us to the end of a stressful day. We gain renewed patience, a fresh sense of humor, and a new surge of creativity and insight by enlisting the aid of the Spirit within us. It's frequently during those late afternoon hours when we most need His extra help.

Ask the Holy Spirit to impart His power and presence to you today, in this very hour. Pray for Him to help you in the ways you need Him most—so you will shine like a diamond under water!

Early to Bed

Most of us are familiar with the old saying: "Early to bed and early to rise, makes a man healthy and wealthy and wise." And there are numerous references in the Bible to the joys and benefits of rising early. The psalmist said,

> *My heart is steadfast, O God, my heart is steadfast;*
> *I will sing and give praise. Awake, my glory!*
> *Awake, lute and harp! I will awaken the dawn.*
> Psalm 57:7-8 NKJV

But what does "awakening the dawn" have to do with our sunset hours? Practically speaking, to rise early in the morning, we have to get to bed early. According to modern sleep research, most people need seven to ten hours of sleep a day, and lost hours can never be made up.

Sufficient sleep is the foremost factor in a person's ability to perform well, cope with stress, and feel a sense of satisfaction in life. Sleep directly impacts our moods and emotions, our ability to think creatively and respond quickly, and our ability to sustain exertion. It is as vital to our health as what we eat and drink.

A good night's sleep is one of God's blessings to you. When you make a habit of retiring early, you put yourself in a position to receive this blessing. You'll find it easier to rise early and seek the Lord for wisdom and strength for the day ahead.

O GOD, YOU ARE MY GOD;

EARLY WILL I SEEK YOU.

PSALM 63:1 NKJV

Talk with the Creator

"There is literally nothing that I have ever wanted to do, that I asked the blessed Creator to help me do, that I have not been able to accomplish. It's all very simple if one knows how to talk with the Creator." So said George Washington Carver, the American botanist who literally rebuilt the southern agricultural economy after the Civil War.

Born a slave, Carver eventually headed the Agriculture Department at Alabama's Tuskegee Institute. He developed hundreds of uses for peanuts and dozens of products from sweet potatoes and soybeans. Much of Carver's research was conducted in his laboratory, which he called "God's Little Workshop."

Carver had a habit of rising at four o'clock every morning to walk in the woods and talk to God. He said, "There He gives me my orders for the day. I gather specimens and listen to what God has to say to me."[17]

You can begin each day asking God what He would have you do that day and how He would have you do it! If you are facing a challenge, He can reveal a new perspective. If you need inspiration, He can stir you up. If you feel you are in a dead-end situation, God can show you His way out.

Seek your Creator today! He desires your fellowship, and He wants to give you the answers you need.

WISDOM BEGINS WITH RESPECT FOR
THE LORD; THOSE WHO OBEY HIS
ORDERS HAVE GOOD UNDERSTANDING.

PSALM 111:10 NCV

Hold On!

A little girl, nervous about her first horseback ride with her grandfather, began to cry as her parents lifted her onto the horse. "I don't know how to ride a horse! I haven't done this before! What do I do?" she wailed.

Her grandfather, an experienced horseman, said reassuringly, "Don't worry about riding the horse, darlin', just hold on to me."

What good advice! We all experience those unexpected "bucking-bronco" days. At times like that, we need to "just hold on" to our faith in the Lord and stay in the saddle.

One important way to hold on to the Lord is through constant communication with Him—a continual flow of prayer and praise. We can pray in any place at any time. Even a "thought" prayer turns our will and focus toward the Lord and puts our trust in Him. But when we lose touch with Him, we risk "falling" into panic and the frustration, frenzy, and failure that can come with it.

God knows the end from the beginning of each day, and He knows how long the current upheaval in your life will last. Above all, He will bring you safely through each "wild ride," keeping you in His divine peace all the way. Just hold on!

PRESERVE ME, O GOD,

FOR IN YOU I PUT MY TRUST.

PSALM 16:1 NKJV

THIS BOOK OF THE LAW SHALL NOT DEPART OUT
OF THY MOUTH; BUT THOU SHALT MEDITATE THEREIN DAY
AND NIGHT, THAT THOU MAYEST OBSERVE TO DO
ACCORDING TO ALL THAT IS WRITTEN THEREIN:
FOR THEN THOU SHALT MAKE THY WAY PROSPEROUS,
AND THEN THOU SHALT HAVE GOOD SUCCESS.

JOSHUA 1:8

Constant Meditation

The Hebrew translation for the word "meditate" is the verb "to mutter"—to continually repeat something under one's breath. In learning to meditate God's Word day and night, we should repeat it to ourselves continually. This way His Word becomes foremost in our thinking and our perspective on life.

In the opinion of Henry Ward Beecher, "A few moments with God at that calm and tranquil season, are of more value than much fine gold."

Make your first conscious thoughts in the morning and last thoughts before sleeping about God's Word. You'll find it easier to do this if you choose a passage of scripture on which to meditate in the morning, and then meditate upon it all day—repeating phrases and verses to yourself in the odd moments of your schedule. Then just before you fall asleep, remind yourself one final time of God's truth.

Those who do this report a more restful mind, peaceful sleep, and deep relaxation for the body. In this day and age, with nearly a billion dollars spent each year on relaxation aids, we have the greatest aid of all—the Word of God!

References

ndnotes

1 Kenneth W. Osbeck, *101 More Hymn Stories* (Grand Rapids, MI: Kregel Publications, 1985)

2 Robert Van de Weyer, ed., *Book of Prayers* (New York, NY: Harper Collins, 1993)

3 Ron Rand, "Won by One," Max Lucado, ed., *The Inspirational Study Bible* (Dallas, TX: Word, 1995)

4 Hazel Fellemen, ed., *The Best-Loved Poems of the American People* (New York, NY: Doubleday, 1936)

5 Toyohiko Kagawa and other Japanese poets, Lois J. Erickson, trans., *Songs from the Land of Dawn* (New York, NY: Friendship Press, 1949)

6 Jamie Buckingham, *The Last Word* (Plainfield: Logos, 1978)

7 Rueben P. Job and Norman Shawchuck, eds., *A Guide to Prayer for All God's People* (Nashville, TN: Upper Room Books, 1990)

8 John Barnett, *Carlsbad Caverns: Silent Chambers, Timeless Beauty* (Carlsbad, NM: Carlsbad Caverns-Guadalupe Mountains Association, 1981)

9 Tony Campolo, "Who Switched the Price Tags?" Max Lucado, ed., *The Inspirational Study Bible* (Dallas, TX: Word, 1995)

10 James W. Hewett, ed., *Illustrations Unlimited* (Wheaton, IL: Tyndale, 1988)

11 Louis Haskins, "Introduction," Mrs. Charles Cowan, ed., *Traveling Toward Sunrise* (Grand Rapids, MI: Zondervan, [no pub date])

12 Tyron Edwards, *The New Dictionary of Thoughts* (New York, NY: Standard, 1963)

13 Patricia Gentry, *Teatime Collections* (San Ramon, CA: Chevron Chemical, 1988)

14 Billy Graham, *Unto the Hills: A Devotional Treasury* (Waco, TX: Word, 1986)

15 *Good Housekeeping,* February 1996.

16 Billy Graham, *Unto the Hills: A Devotional Treasury* (Waco, TX: Word, 1986)

17 Glenn Park, *The Man Who Talks with the Flowers* (St. Paul, MN: Macalester, 1939)

Additional copies of this book and other titles
in the Quiet Moments with God Devotional series
are available from your local bookstore.

Clothbound devotionals:

Breakfast with God   Coffee Break with God
Sunset with God   Tea Time with God
Daybreak with God   Through the Night with God
In the Garden with God   In the Kitchen with God
Christmas with God

Portable gift editions:

Breakfast with God   Coffee Break with God
Sunset with God   Tea Time with God

If you have enjoyed this book, or if it has impacted your life,
we would like to hear from you. Please contact us at:

Honor Books
Department E
P.O. Box 55388
Tulsa, Oklahoma 74155

Or, by e-mail at info@honorbooks.com

Tulsa, Oklahoma